LPA

Meaningful Places and Spaces

First published in Australia in 2000 by
The Images Publishing Group Pty Ltd
ACN 059 734 431
6 Bastow Place, Mulgrave, Victoria, 3170
Telephone (61 3) 9561 5544 Facsimile (61 3) 9561 4860
Email: books@images.com.au
Web Site: www.imagespublishing.com.au

National Library of Australia Cataloguing-in-Publication Data

LPA: meaningful places and spaces.

Includes Index.
ISBN 1 876907 21 5

1. LPA (Firm). 2. Architecture–United States.
3. Interior Design–United States.
4. Landscape Architecture–United States.

729.0973

Final edit by Otmar Miller Consultancy Pty Ltd, Australia
Designed by group c INC New Haven/Boston (BC, EZ)
Production by The Graphic Image Studio Pty Ltd, Mulgrave, Australia
Film by Pageset Pty Ltd, Australia
Printed by Leefung–Asco Printers

LPA

Meaningful Places and Spaces

CONTENTS

INTRODUCTION
MEANINGFUL PLACES
AND SPACES

Dan Heinfeld, FAIA
2000

We live in a world that has become extraordinarily homogenized. The general acceptance of standardized consumer products, the trend towards chain retailers occupying every street corner, and the explosive growth of planned communities give a sense of sameness to our cities. Yet, the precedent for making places and spaces that are unique, or that could only be designed for a specific region or site, is uniquely American: our practical nature made us respond to climate, site conditions, and material availability. Only in recent decades have places become difficult to distinguish from one another.

At LPA, creating places and spaces that enrich the lives of the people who use them is the foundation of our work. We believe that every building can and should engage itself in a dialogue with the history, beliefs, and needs of a particular place and time. LPA's collaborative process to discover a sense of community is driven by the beliefs and values of our firm:

- **Collaborative Engagement**
  Through extensive dialogue and serious engagement with the client, we strive to understand their needs and program. We believe that if we carefully listen to our clients, we will achieve a profound understanding of their dreams, resulting in an architecture that endures.

- **Context as Abstract Imagery**
  We believe that architecture can be a historical and cultural artifact, yielding an increased awareness of local identity.

- **Holistic Narrative**
  Within the practical boundaries of budget and program, we invest the building with a poetic quality—a holistic metaphor that reflects the specific place, time, and values of the people who live there.

Our clients often ask at the very beginning of a project, "Well, what is it going to look like?" We understand the excitement about making a new building, and our clients have the rare opportunity to help us discover the look of their project through this collaborative process. LPA views the design process as a journey, where exploring and listening for inspiration give all projects a unique sense of history. Our process results in a story about the client and the context—past, present, and future inextricably linked.

COLLABORATIVE ENGAGEMENT

Collaborative engagement involves being receptive to new ideas in a process of shared discovery. LPA has found that even the most casual remark by a client can be the source of inspiration that leads the project and suddenly reveals the essence of the place. The process is a creative environment in which everyone feels free to contribute ideas at any time, whether in a full-scale, collaborative meeting or during a ten-minute brainstorming session.

SAGE HILL SCHOOL

The parents who founded Sage Hill School, the first non-denominational, private high school in Orange County, told us they admired the collegiate atmosphere of East Coast college prep academies. They believed that atmosphere helped foster the dialogue between small groups of students and teachers. Given a spacious, hilltop setting and the mild climate of Orange County, we designed a campus in which outdoor as well as indoor space function as part of the educational program. The campus is a series of buildings placed around an upper and lower courtyard that maximizes the play of light and the use of indoor/outdoor space. This spacious campus, coupled with the topography of the site, lends itself to the imagery of a hill town; not in the most literal sense, but an adapted image that speaks of a 21st-century teaching environment where the Internet and flexible classrooms go hand in hand in making a place for learning. Hearing the parents so passionately speak of the need for a sense of permanence to the school led us to design a "foundation" wall as an organizing element for the entire campus. The stone used on the foundation wall is the same color as the rock outcropping on the site, a feature which binds the project to the site. The project is punctuated with a 60-foot tower, which is capped with a translucent material and lit from within; a visible symbol of the past meeting the future.

CONTEXT AS ABSTRACT IMAGERY

Southern California is known for its theme parks and movie sets, which recast historical epochs as glossy spectacles. LPA believes that architecture, unlike entertainment venues, is built to endure for generations. We strive for an authentic interpretation of the history of a place. A historical "dig" on the region, its local influences, and its social and physical culture: each of these can be integrated into the building. Neither flashy nor self-effacing, our buildings embrace and assimilate local influences, reintroducing the value of "the place between." This approach involves abstracting and reinterpreting the past in a meaningful way as a bridge to a contemporary experience.

TEMECULA LIBRARY

The City of Temecula has long been associated with hot air balloon rides and wineries. The design of the Temecula Library is an opportunity to teach the residents about their community's unique heritage. A long, linear site stretched atop a hillside overlooking the Temecula Valley is the perfect setting for this new facility. Borrowing from the Native American folklore of the area, the linear nature of the site is a metaphor for the original journey to find the Temecula Valley. Through pavement, landscape and art installations, the journey will be abstracted through the narrow parking lot, and will terminate into what will be known as the "Temecula Room". Housed within this room will be historically significant art, documents, and literature, all of which will reinforce the heritage of the Temecula Valley. When initially discovered, the Temecula Valley was distinguished because of its unique quality of light. The Native Americans called it "The Valley of the Sun through the Mist." The library itself will become an abstraction of this diffused light quality. Through careful orientation and light monitors, the public as well as the private spaces will shape and form the natural light to produce dramatic interior spaces. The new library will make a contemporary statement using the local history and heritage as building blocks to educate a community about its unique past.

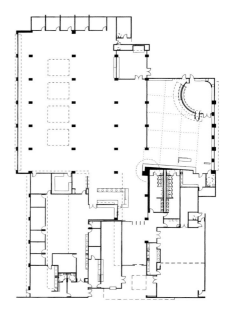

HOLISTIC NARRATIVE

Each of our projects embodies a different narrative that is unique to the personalities of its users and the ambiance of its site. The building tells a story that is both easily perceivable to the viewer and meaningful to the users. This narrative provides a visual program that elevates the work beyond a mere engineering solution, and celebrates our basic needs for beauty and attachment to place. Reflecting qualitative as well as quantitative needs, our buildings yield a sense of discovery—knowledge not only about the users and the function of the building, but also about the community and its place in the world.

FORD MOTOR COMPANY PREMIER AUTOMOTIVE GROUP

When the Ford Motor Company decided to move the North American headquarters of the Premier Automotive Group to a master planned business community known as the "Spectrum" in Irvine, California, four very diverse and individually important companies came together to form one group. LPA was given the task of creating a "narrative" for the project that not only announced the Premier Automotive Group but also recognized the individual luxury brands under the Ford umbrella.

From the very beginning, we were interested in making the building reflect the power of the Premier Automotive Group's diversity, where different elements come together to form a new and stronger organization. The building's main form is a symbol of that plurality. The strong rectangular form of the office building is contrasted at the entry with a soft curve form, which takes its cues from the lines of the car products that the group manufactures. This dialogue also reinforces the context of its place: the form and fenestration of the office building complies with the design guidelines of the business park, while the linear curve of the entry element tells a specific story about the users of the building.

The second part of the project's narrative was a gift from the site—a long linear parcel of land along a major freeway—which gave us an opportunity to abstractly express movement, using a rhythm pattern across the entire site. The site is bounded on the freeway by two overpasses: one to the east and the other to the west. This well-defined boundary gave us the backdrop to create a strong pattern of 30-foot rhythms which would tie the entire 1,500-foot frontage together. The pattern, which carries through the design center and parking structures, intensifies at the office tower which punctuates the tallest part of the project. This pattern creates an abstraction of movement that is symbolic of the nature of this company: a progressive and dynamic company recognized as one of the leaders in its industry.

ONE
VENTURE

Irvine, California
1991

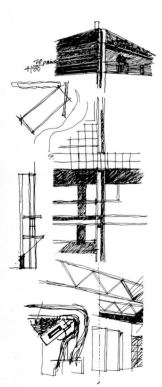

One Venture is a speculative office building that pays homage to the California case study houses of the 1950s, in which modern architecture was interpreted for the climate in California. This was not the type of building that could be understood immediately—it was not to be a non-descript box where one part would make the whole quickly understandable.

The building is positioned on the site to take advantage of solar orientations. Depending on the orientation, the character of the building changes. On the north side, the building is totally open, with its primarily glass front allowing light to pour in. The south side is a series of protective elements: sun screens, overhangs, patterned glass—all are manipulated to protect the glass. The east and west are more closed, using a glass pattern to filter the light through those spaces. Throughout the building, there is always an expression of its physical structure.

The secondary stair is easily accessed from the lobby, which encourages people to walk up to the second floor instead of using the elevator. The lobby functions as a lantern that opens to the visitor parking area, and serves as an indoor/outdoor room. The analogy is carried further with the use of wood furniture that would be typically seen outside in a park element.

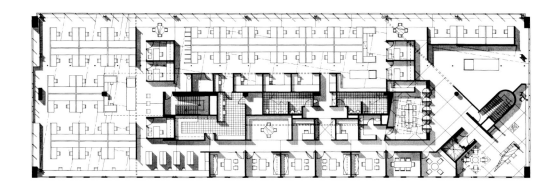

The conference space was meant to be flexible—the pivot doors, with the adjacent circulation, allow the space to grow or close down depending on the need. The projection room, which houses the projection equipment for the conference room, is an extension of one of the pavilions. It recalls the elements visible throughout the building.

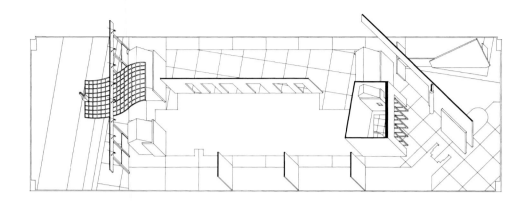

The wave pattern in the ceiling grid connects with the 'pier wall,' forming a metaphor for the California coast.

The interior of the building recalls three of the major California landscapes: the mountains are represented by skewed walls, rising out of the floor element; an agricultural grid and its associated farm buildings are abstracted into the pitched elements within the interior landscape; and finally, the pier, the wave (which hides the mechanical), and the carpet pattern which gets denser and tighter as it approaches the pier, symbolize the ocean and the motion of waves.

Off-the-shelf industrial grates are used to protect the clear glass on the southern side. Coupled with the exposed structural grid, the façade reveals a rich pattern of shadows created by the building components.

Unlike most speculative office buildings, One Venture deals with its context and orientation to tell a narrative about the people who will use the building.

———

KUBOTA
TRACTOR
CORPORATION

Torrance, California
1993

Kubota is a Japanese–American company that manufactures tractors, farm equipment, and hand-scale equipment. We wanted the building to reflect this company's product and its heritage, and to serve as a metaphor for their products. The centrally located "engine" of the building is the research and development portion. The office component, constructed of smooth, metal panels, wraps that R&D "engine"—not unlike the tractor's shell wraps its engine.

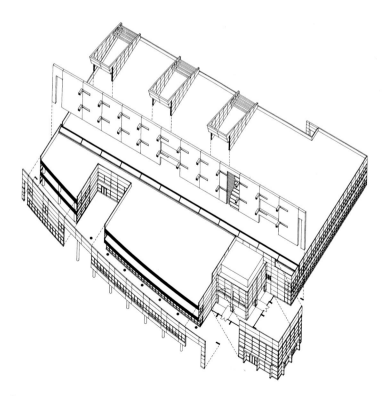

The central space is a display area for some of the first tractors that Kubota imported from Japan to the United States.

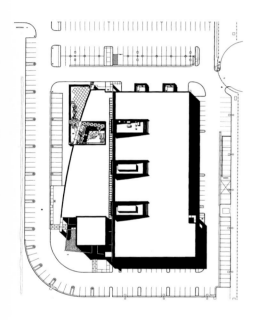

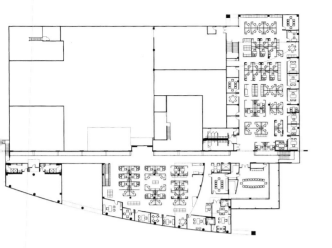
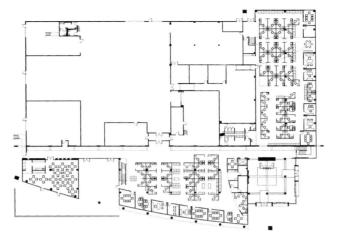

The major circulation spine ties the office work spaces with the corporate amenities, such as the cafeteria and the physical fitness center, and separates them from the research and development functions. Cast in the tilt-up wall are three different abstractions of landscapes, symbolic of how Kubota cultivates the land with its products.

The main conference room overlooks the lobby, in which equipment is displayed to serve as a visible company history. Furthering the historical connection, the shape of the conference room is taken from traditional Japanese building forms. The wood used in this space signifies the human experience, where people come together to talk and make decisions, contrasting with the concrete and hard materials used in the manufacturing portion of the building.

With the main conference space, the intent was to create a transparency between the outside and the inside— that the strong shapes would recall from the inside what you had seen on the outside, and vice versa.

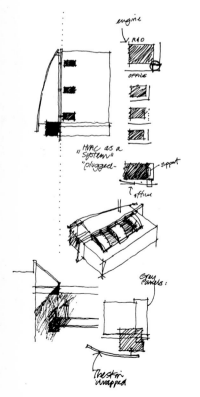

Drawing upon Japanese tradition, a series of Shoji screens create soft, diffused light during the day, sliding partially or completely open to let in direct light.

The series of planes are a conscious framing device throughout the building. Entering the building, there is a literal passage through the planes; looking back through them, they are experienced again as primary forms and as visual frames for the natural environment.

The large stone elements on the ground symbolize the traditional rock base of the Japanese building style. The "Japanese garden" is meant to be a place where employees can have a protected public space of their own. It becomes a mental and physical resting spot—entering into the space gives the feeling of leaving the stress of work behind. It also acts as a visual respite, a place to look upon from both the workspace and the cafeteria.

SAN MARCOS
TOWN CENTER

San Marcos, California
1994

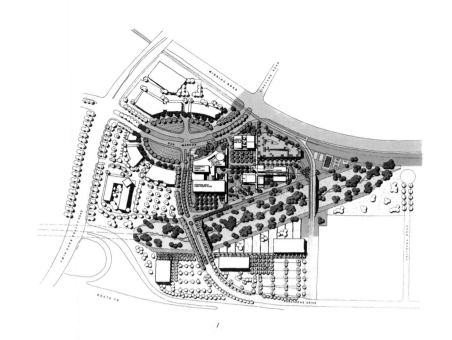

Founded in 1960, the San Marcos city government was still operating from its original, temporary trailer offices and had never really developed a downtown area, a place in which the community could gather. This project was at the heart of the city, and our intent was to create a presence for the city government. A library, community center, and city hall were developed. Within the city hall, spaces for commercial lease lend an entrepreneurial spirit to the area.

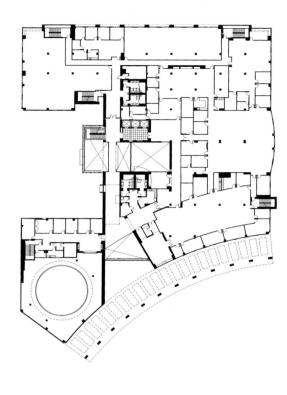

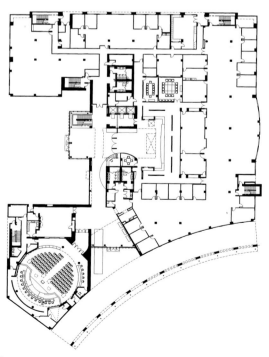

The oval shape on the arterial road and the central civic space, which can be closed off for large-scale events, was designed to be a gathering place for the people of San Marcos. The civic center and the courtyard are centered on a vista that aligns with Mt. Whitney, which becomes the borrowed landscape to that courtyard. The use of the landscape arbor to tie buildings together furthers the idea of integrating the landscape with the structures.

In our discussions with the residents of San Marcos about what they wanted their City Hall to feel like, it became clear that being connected to the landscape at large was very important to them. The design of the project addressed this desire by minimizing the barriers between indoor and outdoor. The use of the natural materials took its cues from the geography of the surrounding valley.

The council chambers were formed to keep an informal and intimate space where the public and its government meet to conduct the city's business. The domed room, where lights and audio visual equipment become stars and moons under a blue sky, takes its visual cues from the adjacent Palomar Observatory.

The placement of the Community Center is designed to create a variety of indoor and outdoor spaces for performance and cultural activities. The outdoor amphitheater shares the same style as the main auditorium, which allows the community to take full advantage of the Southern California climate.

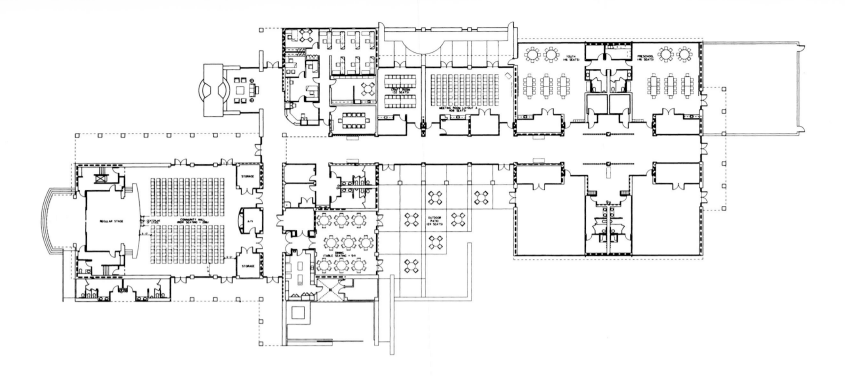

The major pedestrian link from the City Hall to the Community Center is on axis with the indoor/outdoor fireplace bordering the public courtyard.

The fireplace in the Community Center becomes the focal point in the garden. This public courtyard was designed as the gathering space for public events and ceremonies. A landscape arbor ties the three-building complex together, forming a city-scaled courtyard.

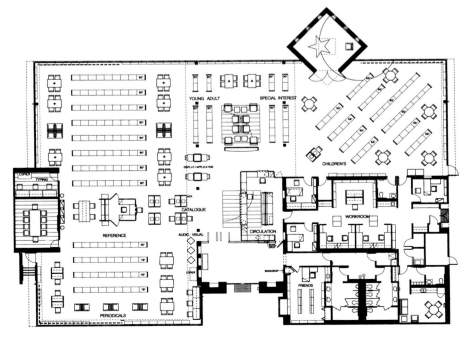

The library is the most public of the three buildings, and is prominently located on the site. The northern orientation facing the arterial road allowed us to create an open transparency to the library that allowed the public to see into the space. The lantern quality at night highlights the importance this community places on personal quest for knowledge.

The story-telling room is an abstract fort designed with seating that can be custom arranged for the story.

DWP TELECOMMUNICATIONS HEADQUARTERS
AND AMTRAK COMMUTER STATION

Van Nuys, California
1995

Continuity between the two buildings is visible in the roof forms, the roofing materials, and the contemporary vocabulary of both buildings. These elements identify the buildings as special within the public community.

The Amtrak train station and Department of Water and Power (DWP) Telecommunications Headquarters in Van Nuys were two public projects located on the same street. The projects were undertaken at the same time, less than two miles apart, for two separate clients. These two projects, on one of the oldest commercial streets in the San Fernando Valley, gave us an opportunity to make each more powerful, to engender a dialogue between them, and to announce these public buildings within their commercial setting. It then became an opportunity to create a larger urban planning gesture for these two small public works.

The Amtrak Commuter Station is surrounded by large-scale public pieces, such as bridges and freeway signs. It responds to the surrounding infrastructure, rather than to individual buildings. It is sculptural, as though the windows were carved out of one piece of material.

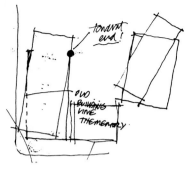

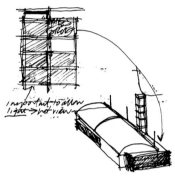

There are similar shapes to the buildings—from the street they immediately stand out from the flat-roofed commercial strip centers surrounding them. The station and the telecommunications headquarters were meant to be public buildings, which announce themselves within their neighborhood.

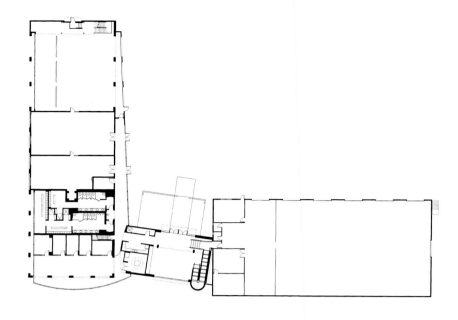

While the buildings bring new forms and materials to an older area of the city, the street façade of the DWP building recalls the brick veneer of the existing context.

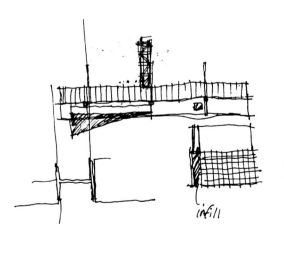

The lobby greets visitors with a sparse, straightforward use of materials, revealing the required functional nature of the building. The ramp accentuates the space, while solving the grade differential between the new and existing facilities.

The communications tower becomes the major visual identity for the project. Located at the intersection of the plan where the different program elements meet, the tower is a symbol to the community of building function.

ANAHEIM

PLAZA

Anaheim, California
1995

Anaheim Plaza was the first indoor mall built in Orange County. This renovation project spawned current trends by converting an existing closed mall into an open, outdoor center. We wanted to create a real alternative to the generic strip mall centers, and to develop something that was more authentic to the community. Developed in the 1880s, Anaheim was parceled in small, two-acre farms with the intent of creating a self-sufficient community, consisting mainly of vineyards. Incorporating Anaheim's history into the plaza, an abstraction of these arbors houses the signage for the development that addresses the freeway.

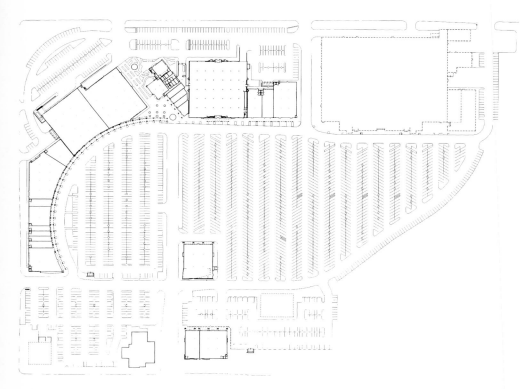

The lighting grid identifies the

entry from the street, and it

counterpoints the delicate

arbor structure by creating a

mass next to it.
———

The signage is meant to be fun and playful, with some agricultural abstractions, such as the leaves that run in and out of the arbor, cast into the tilt-up concrete. In addition, abstractions of oranges as light fixtures indicate the entrance to the food court. The pieces inserted into the arbor also play with shadow and light, both with the natural light and with the grid of lights, ultimately adding another layer to the graphics. The abstracted arbor anchors everything: graphics, pedestrian circulation, individual tenant identification, and the overall plaza signage.

By adding elements into the grid, the standard retail signage is integrated into the arbor. This signage was also accepted by the city as part of the "One Percent for Art" program, which requires that one percent of a project have an art component.

SADDLEBACK VALLEY COMMUNITY CHURCH INTERIM SANCTUARY

Foothill Ranch, California
1995

Saddleback Valley Community Church (SVCC) is one of the largest congregations in California, and possibly the country. The congregation started as a bible study group in 1970, meeting in Pastor Warren's house. When it outgrew the Pastor's house, the congregation moved to the high school gymnasium and held its services there for 15 years. After finding a piece of property, the congragation set up a tent on the site and held services in the tent for two years. When finally it was able to build the Interim Sanctuary, the congregation wanted to recapture the history of its previous meeting places—the gymnasium and the tent.

In California, open space is one of the most precious commodities. The terracing and landscaping anchor this building to the natural landscape and the wilderness and vegetation reserve that is adjacent to the site. The topography was used to create an outdoor amphitheater for special ceremonies and events.

The bridge or pier element becomes a viewing platform to look out into the valley, and is integrated into the ceremonies.

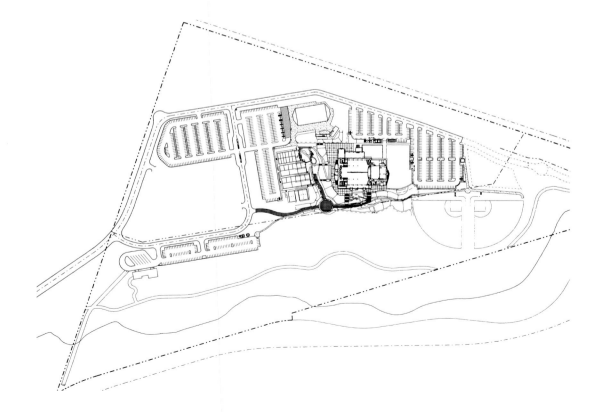

The layering of sun screens allows controlled lighting of the space—it could be protected or opened. As you enter into the church, there is a sense of containment, but then as you proceed, the glass wall opens up with the canopy and series of sun shades.

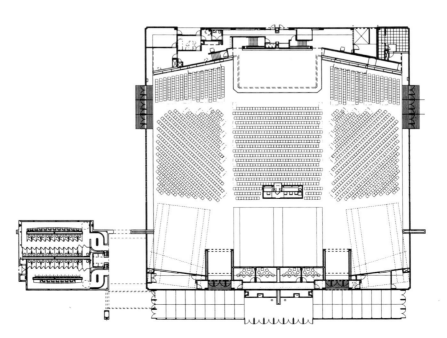

In transition into the large meeting space, the area is open and transparent, filled with light and air—not a traditional church gathering place. One of the tenets of pastor is that a church is not created by its meeting space; it is created by the people. The large openings on the northern and southern sides, which literally allow the entire space to be light-reflected, create an open connection with the outside and give the congregation an ability to see everybody, carrying through one of the building blocks of this congregation.

The design of the interior intentionally exposes mechanical and lighting fixtures, and with the bleacher seating, recalls the former meeting space in the gymnasium.

The courtyard becomes the main gathering space after services. Here the chosen words of the "Scripture Wall" surround the congregation which chose these words. The Scripture Wall filters light and creates a transition to the sanctuary entries. The logo of the church abstracted into the terrazzo floor completes the entry to the worship space.

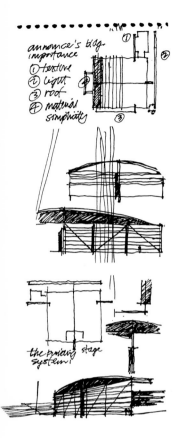

The transparency of the glass
Scripture Wall recalls the thin
enclosure of a tent. Etched
into the glass are important
scriptures that were chosen by
the congregation. Entering into
this glass-walled "tent," you
are surrounded by the words
of the congregation.

THE CHAPEL AT LAKE HILLS COMMUNITY CHURCH

Laguna Hills, California
1997

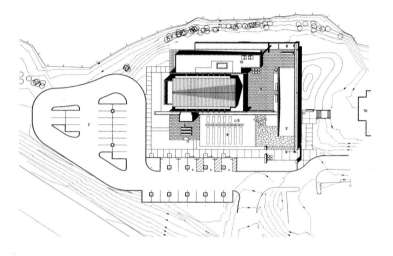

The landscaping works with this building to choreograph a specific arrival procession. A water feature invites you to cross over a bridge element, leaving the world behind before entering into the forecourt of the chapel. That bridge focuses on a natural opening in the eucalyptus trees, which allows views to the water beyond.

The natural refuge of open space and water surrounded by a grove of eucalyptus trees was an inspirational site for this chapel, a gift to the church from a family in honor of their mother. The family spoke of fond memories of their former church in New England, and their desire to convey some of that feeling in this chapel, while specifically responding to the unique Southern California surroundings—'a place to be with God and nature.'

The sense of permanence and warmth of the New England church is conveyed through the use of natural and traditional building materials, such as mahogany and cherry woods and stone. The symmetry of the building recalls the traditional church plan, and the steeple, made of steel channels, is an adaptation of the New England church. Traditional materials and forms interpreted in a contemporary way translate architecture into the church's mission: to be simple, strong, elegant, and timeless.

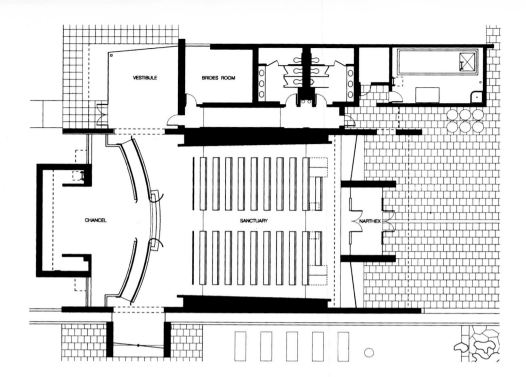

The interior space, highlighted by natural light, is organized to create a crafted feeling of welcome. The furniture, designed by LPA, further enhances the experience.

The rough limestone walls of the chapel contrast with the smooth planar qualities of the wood to create a layering of visual textures. The layers both reveal and conceal the view to the water, and the experience becomes a surprising sequence of glimpsing the surrounding site, losing it, and regaining it. The water and trees of the site visually complete the chapel's interior spaces.

The transparency of the glass creates a sense of a private outdoor room for meditation and prayer, allowing you to be surrounded by the garden without leaving the chapel.

Shaped as a focus and counterpoint to the altar, the railed walkway becomes part of the procession and is integrated into wedding ceremonies.

A private prayer space off the alter offers views into the rose garden. This indoor/outdoor room accentuates the garden, which is used as a congregating space before and after a performance or ceremony.

While the steep pitch of the roof is typical of a New England church, our concern was also with its acoustic performance. In addition to weddings and ceremonies, the space would be home to many live musical performances. The shape of the roof and the wooden walls, along with the angling of the glass in the main façade, were driven by this acoustic intent.

MISSION VIEJO
LIBRARY

Mission Viejo, California
1997

This was the first time the City of Mission Viejo, which was incorporated in 1985, had the opportunity to build a public building. One of the first planned communities in Southern California, Mission Viejo's overriding aesthetic is its earth-colored walls and tile roofs. As the first public building in the city, it was important that the library be contextual, but also differentiate itself within the community.

Because the plaster walls take their color from the surrounding context, the copper-barrel roof over the reading and stack area becomes the signature gesture for the library to proclaim itself as a public building within the community. The exterior reading porches are visible from the street and act as an invitation, welcoming the community inside. The library's site is part of a master plan which includes another public building, a city hall. Together, these two buildings will form a courtyard and gathering space for the entire community.

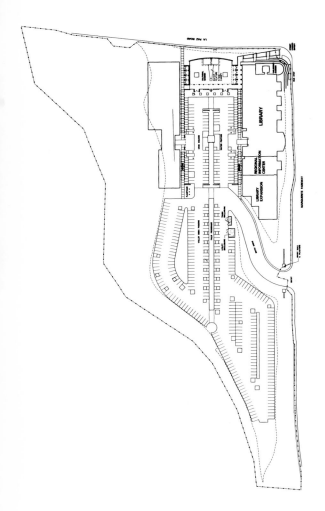

The entry, accented by the public square and a landscape trellis, forms a large outdoor plaza which the community uses for special events. The long, linear site is organized by the Portola Trail, which leads pedestrians from the parking areas.

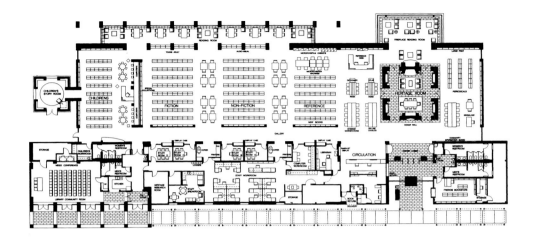

The City of Mission Viejo has a very strong interest in ancestry. The library became a vehicle for enhancing and nurturing this community's interest by creating a "Heritage Room" specifically for ancestral research.

The Sheri M. Butterfield Community Room is equipped with video conferencing capability, enabling the community for distance learning.

The children's wing is specially equipped with workstations that are ergonomically corrected for children using computers.

Collaborative work rooms allow for acoustical privacy while being visually open. Local artwork is displayed along the gallery.

With constellations drawn on the ceiling and low windows looking out to the garden area, we tailored the room specifically to be a fun place for children. We also wanted to acknowledge the history of the city prior to the Spanish Colonial period, and thus the reading room is an abstraction of a *wickiup*, a typical Native American sheltering hut structure. The children's reading room is also visible from the exterior, symbolizing the importance of the children in the community.

MOSSIMO CORPORATE HEADQUARTERS

Irvine, California
1997

Our challenge was to give this cutting-edge clothing company a solution that meshed with its philosophy and still remained within the developer's guidelines and cost structure. To this standard space we added landscape elements, entry pieces, and shading/shadow textures to differentiate this building on the exterior. The atmosphere upon entering is gallery-like, creating a quiet backdrop for the displayed clothing and graphics. The building itself really became a place to display fashion.

Mossimo's designs rely on the tonality of materials and colors, and we wanted the building to reflect that. Contrasted with simple materials and delicate textures and tones throughout, the cherry wood accent desks and their backlit translucent glass become unexpected discoveries within this space.

A major component of the interior is the lighted runway that intersects the major circulation space and the looping display area. This constantly changing, gallery-like display keeps employees updated as projects throughout the company evolve, and serves as a product showcase for visitors.

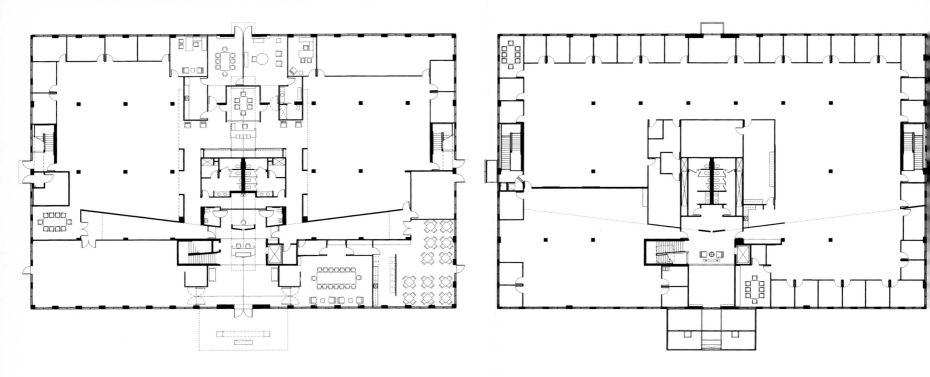

TARBUT V'TORAH
COMMUNITY DAY SCHOOL

Irvine, California
1997

Tarbut V'Torah is a kindergarten through 12th grade Jewish day school. Approximately 50 percent of the faculty are from Israel, and the founders of the school wanted to retain Israel as the spiritual homeland.

We based the plan of the school on the city of Jerusalem by abstracting the four quadrants of the city, the Western Wall, and Temple on the Mount, then organizing the site around them.

The glazing at the multi-story entry to the school administration was meant to be symbolic to the Jewish community. The tower is an abstraction of a menorah, in the glazing pattern of seven panels. There is a play of light between the horizontal volumes and planes that lead you into this taller vertical space, creating compression that is released as you move into the space.

The four parts of the building program support the four different teaching quadrangles: lower primary, upper primary, middle school and high school. These elements are formed around a courtyard which became the protected space for the students. The textured concrete block wall is symbolic of the Western Wall, and is the key organizational element of the overall development.

The interior courtyard is a gathering space for up to 600 people. Various functions are held there, including special holiday and religious ceremonies. The massive stone architectural furniture operate as dividers, as well as playscapes and benches for children. They were designed with these multiple uses in mind, and allow the children to transform this geography.

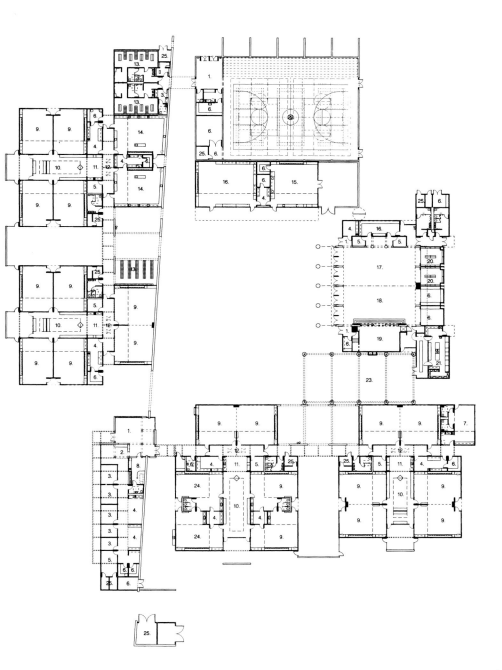

The Jerusalem stone, purposely used only at the entry, identifies this as a special place.

Jewish architecture is always adapted to the site. In Catholicism, the missionaries built identical churches in every location, but Jewish architecture is about the community context and being suited to its place.

The desert-like climate of Southern California is similar to the climate of Israel. In looking at ways to protect the openings from heat and sun, we played with shade and shadow to create openings in a sensitive way. The solid walls were an important part of this, and are also important components in Middle Eastern Judaic buildings.

The five columns in front of the multi-purpose room are symbolic of the five *Torah* books written by Moses, and the barrel vault is an acknowledgement of the architecture in the old parts of Jerusalem. The shape of the roof identifies the multi-purpose room as an important public place. This is the space where people come from outside the school to attend events, and this was seen as a very important rallying building for the Jewish community. In creating the referential layers, we acknowledged the importance of this culture within the community.

The trellis, reminiscent of the roof-top patios of Jerusalem, filters natural light into the computer room from above and protects the computer screens from glare.

The grid of the palms forms an oasis. The idea of placing them in a grid came from one of the student groups. All of the classes were asked to draw and write short articles about what they saw as the ideal biblical garden. One of the drawings illustrated a grid of palm trees with the principal and students learning under them.

CALIFORNIA STATE UNIVERSITY CHANCELLOR'S OFFICE

Long Beach, California
1999

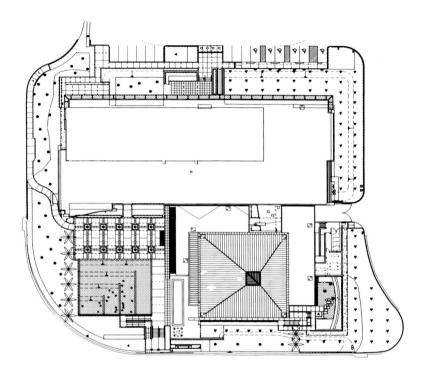

Although no single moment in time is adequate to define the founding of California State University (CSU), which has many milestones, CSU became an independent system in 1961. Today it is one of the largest university systems in the country. As a consistently growing and evolving institution, the CSU wanted to consolidate a number of different work groups into a more efficient, highly flexible office building, and to maintain a presence in Long Beach on the same site as its original facility. As the headquarters for an organization that is responsible for a large portion of capital projects in the State, we felt that this building should set an example for the system with regard to good design practice that can be attained without relying merely on technology. To that end, the overall aesthetic is a response to the building's orientation and the expression of the program elements.

The site configuration led to six efficient floor plates of 24,000 square feet, which afford the organization a highly flexible plan for future changes in operating functions. Based on program requirements and a desire in the organization to create a more open attitude, the floor plan was offset, placing offices toward the center and open workspaces toward the windows, thereby maximizing the area which shares the view of the ocean to the south.

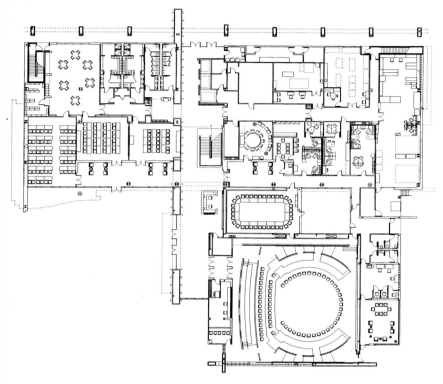

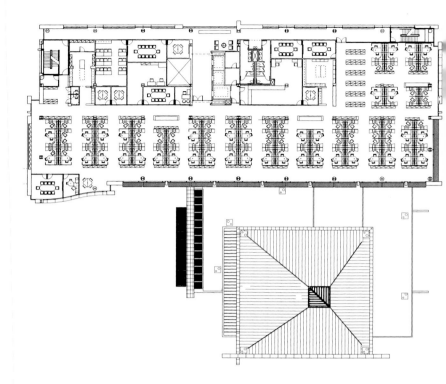

The conference center, which requires off-hour access and an increased ceiling height, is located immediately adjacent to the access road and all visitor parking. Visually separate from the main building, this space is further accentuated by a translucent "sail" which allows light into the space during the day and is a lantern to visitors at night.

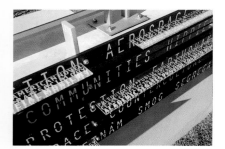

The open space is used as an extension of the program areas for special events that are regular functions at the facility. The area immediately south of the building complex, where the previous building stood, was formed into a "Trustee Park," which incorporates the existing large canopy of trees with an abstract meridian grid to geographically locate all 23 campuses in the system.

A natural amphitheater west of the conference center is accentuated by a water feature with 1,000 bubble jets; symbolic of the University's nickname "The 1,000-mile University." The grass area to the west of the water feature is a symbolic timeline which marks the founding date of each campus. Each segment of time has a series of events and important issues inscribed on a sign bar to help place the founding of the campus in time. The cultural and social events timelines were part of a system-wide study by selected faculty, students, and administrators.

Throughout the Trustee Park, individual light posts represent each campus in the CSU system. Positioned geographically amongst the abstract meridian grid, each campus marker is inscribed with the name of the campus it represents, the date it was founded, and important events in that campus's history. The lights atop each fixture communicate with each other in Morse Code, flashing the letters C–S–U. With icons such as these, we have created a meaningful place for the people who work there.

SELECTED

CHRONOLOGY

1978

Chapman College Harold Hutton Sports Center
Orange, California

Larkspur Landing
Larkspur, California

1979

Clubhouse V
Laguna Hills, California

1981

Greystone Phase I
Las Vegas, Nevada

1984

Automatic Data Processing (ADP)
La Palma, California

California Center
Sacramento, California

1985

Hutton Center
Santa Ana, California

State Compensation Insurance Fund
Sacramento, California

1986

Tri-City Landing
San Bernardino, California

1987

Pod, Inc.
Santa Ana, California

1988

Calmat Corporate Headquarters
Los Angeles, California

E.R. Squibb & Sons
Irvine, California

River Center
Tuscon, Arizona

Tuscon Gateway
Tuscon, Arizona

DWP Sun Valley Distribution Headquarters
Sun Valley, Arizona

1990

AST Research Corporate Headquarters
Irvine, California

Tustin Marketplace
Tustin, California

Vons Corporate Headquarters
Arcadia, California

1991

Disneyland Hotel
Anaheim, California

El Camino Community Center
Orange, California

Natomas Corporate Center
Sacramento, California

One Venture
Irvine, California

1992

Burbank Gateway Center
Burbank, California

Irvine Ranch Water District
Irvine, California

North Island Federal Credit Union
Chula Vista, California

One Parkside
San Bernardino, California

Palomar College Wellness/Fitness Center
San Marcos, California

1993

ASK Computer Corporate Headquarters
Mountain View, California

Bumble Bee Corporate Headquarters
San Diego, California

Continental Retail
El Segundo, California

California State University
School of Business and Information Sciences
San Bernardino, California

Kubota Tractor Corporation
Torrance, California

San Bernardino County Law Library
San Bernardino, California

San Diego Gas and Electric
San Diego, California

Desert Vineyard Christian Fellowship
Lancaster, California

New Venture Christian Fellowship
Oceanside, California

1994

San Marcos Town Center: City Hall
San Marcos, California

San Marcos Town Center: Community Center
San Marcos, California

San Marcos Town Center: Library
San Marcos, California

Temecula Community Recreation Center
Temecula, California

1995

Amtrak Commuter Station
Van Nuys, California

Anaheim Plaza
Anaheim, California

Chula Vista Library
Chula Vista, California

DWP Telecommunications Headquarters
Van Nuys, California

Faith Community Church
West Covina, California

Garden Grove City Hall
Garden Grove, California

Moreno Valley City Hall
Moreno Valley, California

**Saddleback Valley Community Church
Interim Sanctuary**
Foothill Ranch, California

1996

Brea Community Center
Brea, California

Irvine Spectrum Pavilion
Irvine, California

Mission Viejo Town Center
Mission Viejo, California

Playmates Toys, Inc.
Costa Mesa, California

Rancho Bernardo Branch Library
San Diego, California

University Research Park
Irvine, California

1997

Gemological Institute of America (GIA)
Carlsbad, California

The Chapel at Lake Hills Community Church
Laguna Hills, California

1998

Anaheim Community Center
Anaheim, California

Mission Viejo Library
Mission Viejo, California

Mossimo Corporate Headquarters
Irvine, California

Paramount Park K–8 Elementary School
Paramount, California

Tarbut V'Torah Community Day School
Irvine, California

San Juan Capistrano Community Center
San Juan Capistrano, California

Southern California College of Optometry
Fullerton, California

University Montessori
Irvine, California

Toyota Master Plan
Torrance, California

1999

**California State University
Chancellor's Office**
Long Beach, California

Mission Imports
Laguna Niguel, California

Moreno Valley Public Safety Facility
Moreno Valley, California

Santiago Canyon College Learning Resource Center
Orange, California

Running Springs Elementary School
Anaheim, California

Ann Soldo Elementary School
Watsonville, California

2000

Ross/Park Elementary School
Anaheim, California

Sage Hill School
Newport Coast, California

San Diego Jewish Academy
Del Mar, California

STUDIO

Principals

Robert Kupper
Dan Heinfeld
David Gilmore
James Kelly
James Wirick
Chris Torrey
Steven Kendrick
Glenn Carels
Wendy Rogers
Jon Mills
Rick d'Amato
Joseph Yee
Charles Pruitt
James Kisel
Karen Thomas
John Gack
Kevin Sullivan

Associates

Brandon deArakal
Chris Lentz
Young Min
Patrick McClintock
Steven Tiner
Carrick Boshart
Steven Flanagan

Staff

Ken Murai
Lynette Stabile
Laura Nelson
Keith Hempel
Arash Izadi

Lorrie Ellis
Quoc Winston Bao
Mike Lehmberg
John Robison
Geoffrey Chevlin
Damon Dusterhoft
David Duff
Angela Woodward
John Vezirian
Nathaniel Woods
Jamie Heidebrink
Gloria Broming
James Raver
Jon Ludwig
Kimberly Spence
Jean Stolzman
Robert Demmond
Jeffrey Perry
Doug Choi
Maria Mocanu
Daniel Delgado
Jack Wilinski
Chris Arnold
Antoinette Storch
Kimberly Kelly
Julia Becker
Lawrence Chiu
Michael Henning
Leah Zawadzki
Deann Salcido
Jody Stephany
Tracy Ettinger
Lori Cantley
Lisa Luttrell
Gillian Crane

Scott Harper
Jeremy Hart
Laura Goforth
Rebecca Snellen van Vollehoven
Richard Bienvenu
Thomas Morrissey
Traci Maynard
Jacki Williams
Michael Cecconi
Wendy Dailey
Casey Kysoth
Jennifer Holmes
William Beaubeaux
Anthony Bertolini
Radamaes Lamboy
Brian Prock
Anna New
Tonya Howell
Bill Prentice
Krista Nakamura
David Landells
John Dexter Galang
Michelle Wheatley
Doug Cochran
Denise Mendelssohn
Kenneth Taylor
Adam de Leon
Bita Alaghband
Lisa Yasutake
Sherrilyn Arnold
Justin Kerfoot
Yu-Ping Chang
Travis Mahoney
Robert Briseno
Silke Metzler

Christin Martinelli
Allan First
Michael Rich
Donald Richmond
Thomas Hsieh
Mario Hernandez
Dianne Forman
David Diep
James Craig Whitridge
Mark Billing
Peggy Gack
John Cook
Paul Breckenridge
Kim Silva
Judy Blonde
Marc Pange
Richard Garcia
Ron Sorenson
Susan Ordoubadian
Ken Francis
Carol Potter
Annabell Cataldo
Todd Lawrence
Donald Pender
Ana Oushakoff
Jason Dreher
Sheri Bond
Jeanette Ehle
Lili Ludwig
William Lardner
Nicole Patel
Flavio Zuniga
Craig Prestininzi
Jennie Mcdonald
Paul John

Haiyan Ye
Alice Henselman
Craig Shulman
Wendy Crenshaw
Claudia Hernandez
Michael Leighton
Franklyn Huggard
Dave Harvey
Rene Pandeus
Matt Zapata
Chris Larson
Anna Schoon
Chris Saurage
Adrienne Tabo
Brett Houser
David Redden
Robin Bugbee
Laurie Noon
Kimberly Ur
Lindsay Hayward
Sara Shanahan
Kentaro Shibaya
Bill Shapton
Myra Lopez
Laura O'Connor
Karen Folsom
Sandra Guy
Michael McAllister
Ti Thang
Michele Pitts
Shawn Bondly

STUDIO 121

PHOTOGRAPHY CREDITS

FRONT MATTER
> Adrian Velicescu p.3
>
> Timothy Hursley p. 4

INTRODUCTION
> All courtesy of LPA

ONE VENTURE
> Jay Hyma p. 10
>
> Timothy Hursley pp. 11–17
>
> Jay Hyma p. 17, upper right

KUBOTA TRACTOR CORPORATION
> Adrian Velicescu

SAN MARCOS TOWN CENTER
> Timothy Hursley pp. 26–27, 33 lower, 34 lower
>
> David Hewitt/Anne Garrison pp. 28–32, 33 upper, 34 upper, 35 right, 36–39
>
> B. Coffee p.35, left

DWP TELECOMMUNICATIONS HEADQUARTERS AND AMTRAK COMMUTER STATION
> Adrain Velicescu

ANAHEIM PLAZA
> Adrian Velicescu

SADDLEBACK VALLEY COMMUNITY CHURCH INTERIM SANCTUARY
> Timothy Hursley

THE CHAPEL AT LAKE HILLS, COMMUNITY CHURCH
> Timothy Hursley

MISSION VIEJO LIBRARY
> Adrian Velicescu, all except p. 89
>
> Larry Crandall p. 89

MOSSIMO CORPORATE HEADQUARTERS
> Adrian Velicescu

TARBUT V'TORAH COMMUNITY DAY SCHOOL
> Adrian Velicescu

CALIFORNIA STATE UNIVERSITY, CHANCELLOR'S OFFICE
> Adrian Velicescu pp. 106; 108, 111; 112 lower; 114–115
>
> Timothy Hursley pp. 107; 109–110; 112, left; 113

CHRONOLOGY
> Ronald Moore p. 116, left
>
> Jay Hyma p. 116, upper right
>
> Infocus Productions p. 117; 120–121
>
> Adrian Velicescu p. 118
>
> Timothy Hursley p. 119